A special gift for you

To

_____

From

_____

D1053587

Introduction

A woman and her granddaughter were spending time together one day. As often happened, the little girl was plying her grandma with questions. Suddenly, with a very serious tone the girl asked, "Grandma, what happens when you die?"

The woman explained to the best of her ability, but the girl only looked at her in wonder. "Does that mean you won't be here with me anymore?" she asked.

The grandmother nodded and said, "Yes, that is true."

"Does that mean you won't be able to bake cookies with me anymore?" asked the girl.

"Yes," said the grandmother, "it is true."

"Does that mean you won't be able to teach me to sew anymore?"

"Yes," said the woman, "it is true."

"Does it mean you won't be able to take me shopping anymore?" asked the girl.

"Yes," Grandma said, "it is true."

"Well," said the girl, "who will do those things, if you are not here?"

The woman responded, "Honey, when that time comes, it will be time for you to do those things for another little girl."

Yes, the time will come for the next generation to pass it on. Which brings to mind another thought — what will they have from our generation to pass on to the next? What are we leaving behind which will be important enough to pass on to the next generation?

It's a challenge…but will our generation pass along life principles that are so important they will not be discarded by the next? Let's keep at it and not give up.

"Train a child in the way he should go, and when he is old he will not turn from it." — Prov. 22:6

"A grandmother is a *BABYSITTER* who watches the kids instead of the television."

— Unknown

Be fruitful, and multiply. – Gen. 1:28

"It's funny what happens
when you become a grandparent.

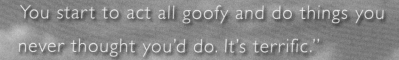

You start to act all goofy and do things you never thought you'd do. It's terrific."

— Mike Krzyzewski

He maketh me to lie down in green pastures: He leadeth me beside the still waters. He restoreth my soul. – Ps. 23:2,3

"God gave us memories

that we might have

roses in December."

—— Sir James M. Barrie

Remember now thy Creator in the days of thy youth, while the evil days come not, nor the years draw nigh, when thou shalt say, I have no pleasure in them . . . – Eccles. 12:1

"The *SIMPLEST* toy, one which even the youngest child can operate, is called a grandparent." — Sam Levinson

And God said, Let the earth bring forth grass, the herb yielding seed, and the fruit tree yielding fruit after its kind, whose seed is in itself, upon the earth: and it was so. – Gen. 1:11

To know the road ahead — ask those COMING BACK."

— Chinese proverb

Receive my sayings; and the years of thy life shall be many. – Prov. 4:10

Colors fade,

temples crumble,

empires fall,

but

WISE

words endure."

— Edward L. Thorndike

I have taught thee in the
way of wisdom; I have led
thee in right paths. – Prov. 4:11

"It's such a

GRAND

thing to be a
mother of a mother
— that's why the
world calls her
grandmother."

— Unknown

Honor and majesty are
before him: strength and
beauty are in his sanctuary.
– Ps. 96:6

"In matters of

PRINCIPLE,

stand like a rock; in

matters of taste, swim

with the current."

— Thomas Jefferson

Tremble, thou earth, at the presence
of the Lord, at the presence of the God
of Jacob; Which turned the rock into a
standing water, the flint into a fountain of
waters. — Ps. 114:8

W ear a *smile* and have friends;

wear a *scowl* and have wrinkles."

— George Eliot

*In the hearts of all that are wise hearted
I have put wisdom.* – Exod. 31:6

*Gray hair is a crown
of splendor; it is
attained by a
righteous life:*

— Prov. 16:31

"A friend of mine was asked how she liked having her first *great-grandchild*. 'It was wonderful,' she replied, 'until I suddenly realized that I was the mother of a grandfather!' "

— Robert L. Rice

To be trusted is a greater compliment than to be loved." — George MacDonald

And his mercy is on them that fear him from generation to generation. – Luke 1:50

"If NOTHING is going well, call your grandmother."

— Italian proverb

But let all those that put their trust in thee rejoice: let them ever shout for joy, because thou defendest them: let them also that love thy name be joyful in thee. – Ps. 5:11

To seek wisdom in old age is like

a mark in the *SAND*;

to seek wisdom in youth is like

an inscription on *S T O N E*."

— Solomon Ben Gabirol

My son, hear the instruction of thy father, and forsake not the law of thy mother.

— Prov. 1:8

A good man leaveth an inheritance to his children's children. — Prov. 13:22

"Grandchildren
are God's way of
COMPENSATING
us for growing old."

– Mary H. Waldrip

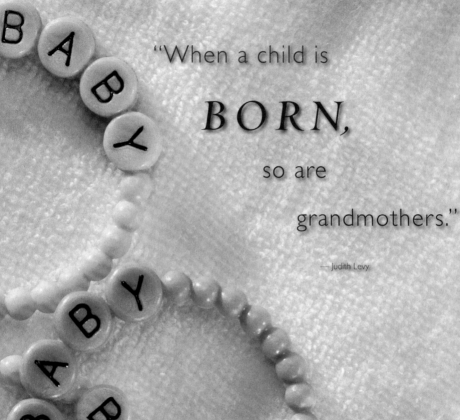

"When a child is **BORN,** so are grandmothers."

— Judith Levy

O clap your hands, all ye people; shout unto God with the voice of triumph.
— Ps. 47:1

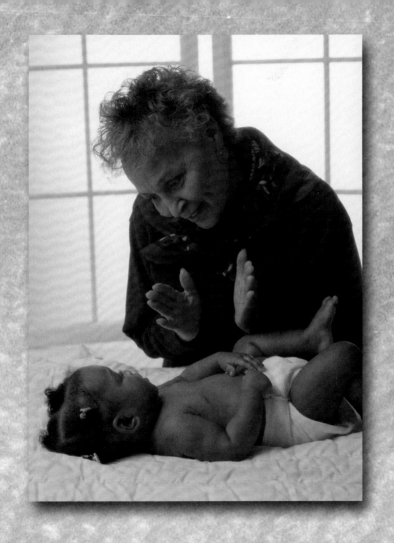

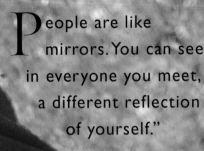

"**P**eople are like mirrors. You can see in everyone you meet, a different reflection of yourself."

— Simon Heighwaya

Let your conversation be without covetousness; and be content with such things as ye have: for he hath said, I will never leave thee, nor forsake thee. — Heb.13:5

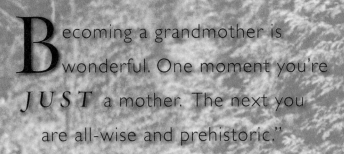

"Becoming a grandmother is wonderful. One moment you're *JUST* a mother. The next you are all-wise and prehistoric."

— Pam Brown

Lead me in thy truth, and teach me: for thou art the God of my salvation; on thee do I wait all the day. -- Ps. 25:5

"Grandmas are moms with lots of  frosting."

— Unknown

Hold fast to that which is good. – I Thess. 5:21

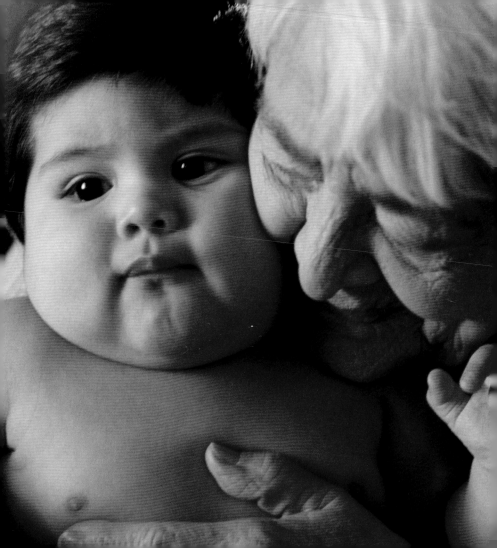

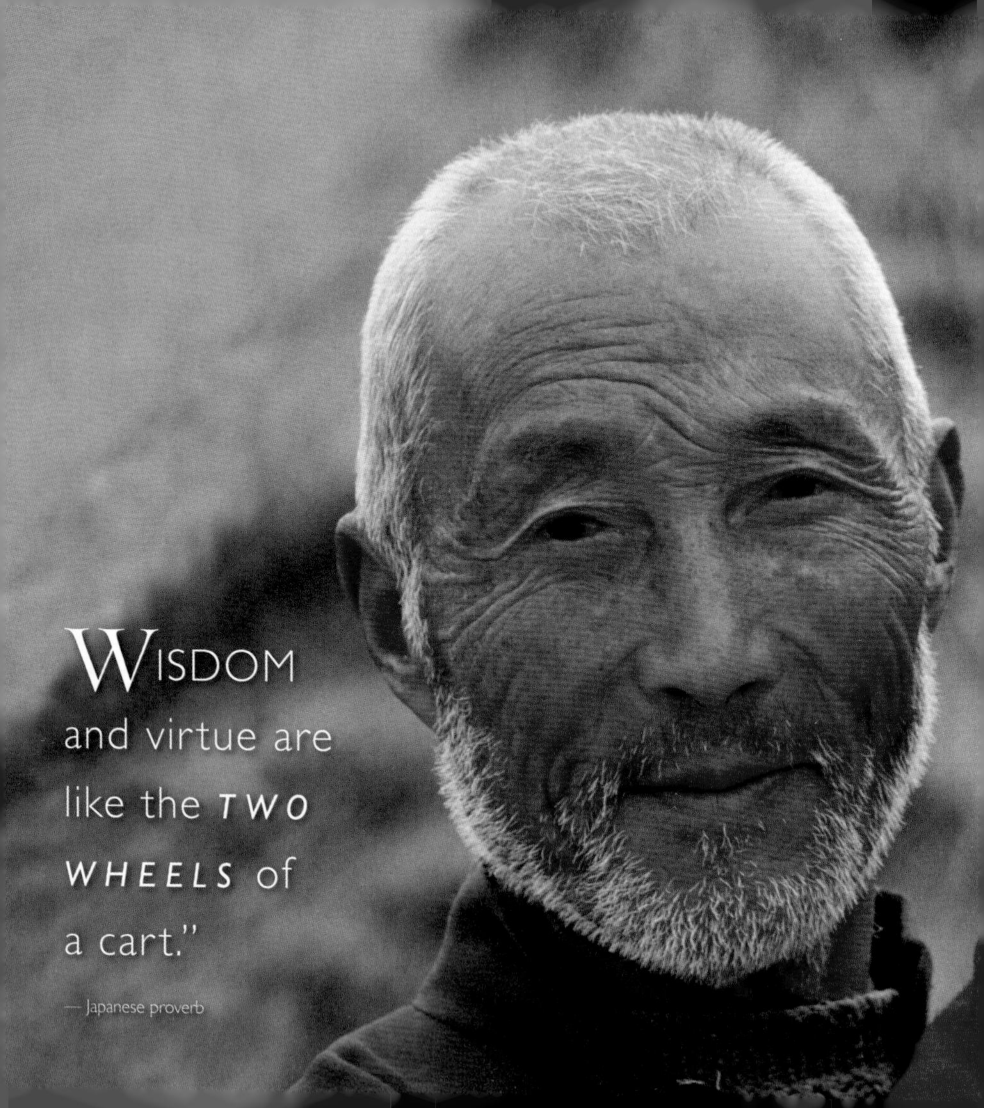

WISDOM
and virtue are
like the *TWO*
WHEELS of
a cart."

— Japanese proverb

Receive my sayings; and the
years of thy life shall be many.
– Prov. 4:10

"A GOOD TEACHER

is one whose
ears get as
much exercise
as his mouth."

— Proverb

I am with thee according to thy heart. – I Sam. 14:7

"**NOBODY** can do for little children what grandparents do. Grandparents sort of sprinkle stardust over the lives of little children." — Alex Haley

Take heed to thyself, and keep thy soul diligently, lest thou forget the things which thine eyes have seen. – Deut. 4:9